Original title:
Through the Keyhole of Time

Copyright © 2025 Creative Arts Management OÜ
All rights reserved.

Author: Tobias Winslow
ISBN HARDBACK: 978-1-80587-204-7
ISBN PAPERBACK: 978-1-80587-674-8

Secrets Beneath the Surface of Time

Tucked away in the attic's gloom,
Old clocks tick softly, dispelling doom.
Grandpa's mischief, preserved in dust,
Knocking over milk, who can we trust?

Rats in tuxedos dance at midnight,
While socks trade secrets by moonlight.
A cat in shades, sipping on tea,
What a world, come and see!

The Chronicles of Lost Moments

Once I lost a sandwich at three,
Sailed it through time, just like a spree.
There it floats, with lettuce aflame,
Cows on roller skates, what a game!

Oh look, there's my sister's old shoe,
Squeaking about like she often flu.
It spins tales of adventure and glee,
Her missing left foot forever free!

Windows to the Worn Past

Peering through glass, I see a chair,
Hunched over with secrets, a past affair.
The dog in pajamas reads the news,
While the goldfish learns to rock and cruise.

Paintings chuckle as they change colors,
They gossip of youngsters, their dreams like hollers.
A broom's lament fills the dusty air,
As it sweeps up memories of laughter and care.

Reflections in the Facets of Time

Mirrors giggle and twist in cheer,
Old Aunt Myrtle winks, then disappears.
A dapper rabbit in a bowler hat,
Invites me for tea with a random cat.

Time's a jester, pulling my leg,
Chasing shadows, dancing a beg.
With each tick, a bubble of fun,
Forever laughing under the sun!

Time's Gentle Caress

Tick-tock goes the clock, what a sight,
A squirrel's dance in the pale moonlight.
Grandpa's tales that twist and twirl,
About his youth and a dancing girl.

Hours race like a bird in flight,
Frogs sing songs of pure delight.
With giggles echoing through the day,
Time's tricks make us laugh and play.

A cat in a hat joins the fun,
Chasing shadows, oh what a run!
Silly moments, they come and go,
Rolling in laughter, what a show.

So let's toast to hours long gone,
With jokes and laughter, we carry on.
Time's gentle tickle, what joy we find,
In the silly antics that life's designed.

The Lost Art of Remembering

Memories flip like pancakes on a griddle,
Silly stories, oh, aren't they a riddle?
Who dropped the cake, who made the mess?
Retelling tales, we all feel blessed.

Old photo albums, a dust-covered shrine,
Where Uncle Joe wore a dress, looking fine.
Reliving moments of grandeur and glee,
When Grandma danced with her pet parakeet.

Poking fun at the bloopers of yore,
We laugh until our sides are sore.
In the chaos of history's embrace,
The lost art of laughter fills the space.

So let's forget the world's narrow grind,
And savor the folly of the past we find.
With a chuckle at life's wild parade,
The art of remembering won't ever fade.

Stories in the Blink of an Eye

In a blink, the world can change,
A cat and a dog, who could arrange?
They plan a scheme to steal a pie,
And up the tree, they dart and fly.

A wizard sneezes, spells go awry,
Turning shoes into clouds in the sky.
With a whoosh and a laugh, they float around,
Such stories in moments, so easily found.

Ticklish fairies in the garden dance,
With sprightly steps, they take a chance.
They spin and twirl under the sun,
Creating laughter where there's no fun.

In a blink, the fun can just ignite,
A jellybean monster gives a fright!
But with giggles and grins, they hold the prize,
In stories that sparkle in our eyes.

The Passage of Dreams

In a land where socks do dance,
Caught in dreams, they take a chance.
Jellybeans float, quite absurd,
Upside down, we fly like birds.

Timmy's watch ticks backwards now,
A cow jumps over a big brown plow.
Laughing clocks all shout `Oh dear!`
Sipping tea with no one near.

The moon plays tag with little stars,
As cats play pianos, strumming guitars.
Lollipops rain down from above,
A world of giggles, full of love.

Splinters of Reality

A fish in a suit with a briefcase too,
Knew the market better than me and you!
He flipped through charts while sipping his tea,
Claiming, 'Stocks are a fin-tastic spree!'

Unicorns joke in the corner shop,
Trading tales, they can't just stop.
With cupcakes that giggle and dance about,
They keep the laughter, there's never doubt.

Time does a jig on a skateboard deck,
As rubber ducks dive with quite a wreck.
Splinters of laughter, fragments of cheer,
Reality's funny, come join us here!

Whispers from the Ether

A lantern ghost floats with a wink,
Cracking jokes as we all think.
It's a party beneath a sunny shade,
Where apples scream and lemons wade.

Balloons get up to share a drink,
While clouds craft tales that make us blink.
Magic hats pull rabbits in glee,
Offering fortune, though none for me.

Elders boast of their wisdom so grand,
But squirrels take over, giving a hand.
Whispers carry laughter and glee,
In this frolicsome world, you see!

The Cycle of Hours

Time flies by on roller skates,
Wearing hats of various states.
A tick-tock rabbit, huge and spry,
Dances just a little too high.

Wednesdays waddle like ducks in line,
While Mondays mix in lemon-lime.
Fridays dance a jig so clever,
Proclaiming, "Oh, we'll party forever!"

The sun throws confetti, what a delight,
While clouds have a pillow fight at night.
A waltzing hourglass spills its sand,
Tickling cheeks with a gentle hand.

When Shadows Dance

In a corner, shadows chuckle,
Twisting tales of the past,
A cat in a hat, quite baffled,
Fleas in a ballet, they dance fast.

Tick-tock goes the silly clock,
Mice play tag, what a shock,
A jester prances with glee,
As laughter echoes, wild and free.

Each moment winks with mischief,
As giggles bounce off the walls,
The ghost in the cupboard mutters,
As confetti from nowhere falls.

So let us twirl with the night,
In a whirlwind of silly glee,
For every shadow has a story,
And they spell it out with tea!

The Book of Forgotten Tomorrows

Dust bunnies dance on the cover,
Of a tome from a whimsy place,
Words flip-flop and stutter,
As we try to keep with the pace.

Once it said we'd fly to Mars,
On a llama in polka dots,
Now it whispers, 'Stay where you are,'
Floating dreams and forget-me-not.

Characters leap off the pages,
Chasing their tails, oh so bold,
Magical recipes and sages,
Cooking up mishaps, untold.

In this quirky, funny realm,
Time's a clown, juggling fate,
A laugh erupts, helm on a helm,
Tomorrow's mess feels just great!

Temporal Threads

Spinning realms with just a laugh,
Threads of time twist and twirl,
A squirrel in a bowler hat,
He plays chess with a swirl.

Each strand a giggle, a jibe,
As time knots in a silly shuffle,
Moments bubble like fizzing bribe,
While we munch popcorn and chuckle.

Past and future wear fun hats,
Dancing in a wobbly line,
Giggling grandmas and feisty cats,
In this silly space of mine.

So tie the bow, let's not whine,
Let's frolic in this knitted delight,
For every tick-tock, there's a sign,
Of joy in the day and night!

Enigmas in the Ether

Whispers float on electric breeze,
Questions bounce with a twinkle,
What's the sound of buzzing bees?
Is it laughter? Or just a wrinkle?

Time itself plays hopscotch here,
With socks that never match,
Twirling secrets without a care,
In jumbled tales, they attach.

A sock puppet claims it can fly,
As it dances and flaps about,
While timekeepers laugh, oh my!
In this realm of jest, no doubt.

So ponder lightly and peek inside,
Fun awaits at every turn,
As enigmas and giggles collide,
In a timeless world where we learn!

Ciphers of the Timeless Realm

In a land where clocks tick backwards,
Every minute's a silly race,
Sneaky seconds wear pajamas,
Making time lose all its grace.

Jokers leap from ticking flowers,
While seconds dance on crooked beams,
The past and future play for hours,
In a world that's stitched with dreams.

Old wizards juggle with their hats,
Telling tales from yo-yos spun,
As funny hats sit on their cats,
Each laugh echoes—what a pun!

The stars slide down in bright balloon,
They giggle loud with cosmic glee,
Chasing shadows with a spoon,
Time's a circus—come and see!

Retracing Steps on Time's Labyrinth

In meandering paths of giggles,
Sneaky socks run with a cheer,
Every twist brings funny wiggles,
Chasing laughter far and near.

Cunning clocks with noses twitch,
Tickle time to make it squeal,
We're all caught in the same glitch,
Where past and future love to wheel.

Echoes of jokes from yesterday,
Bounce around like bouncing balls,
As echoes shout, 'This way, this way!'
The labyrinth dances, never stalls.

Laughter loops like a catchy tune,
As fun hangs on a crooked line,
In this maze where jesters swoon,
Each corner's turned—a new punchline!

The Hourglass of Hidden Visions

Inside the glass, grains tumble down,
Wearing tiny party hats,
In this fun-filled, time-worn town,
Every second plays at spats.

Chasing shadows of old galas,
Where time forgot to wear its shoes,
Dancing clocks sip on sweet teas,
Cracking jokes and sharing views.

With a wink, the hourglass grins,
Changing seconds into fun,
It knows that laughter always wins,
When the ticking's said and done.

So let's swirl in a whirl of glee,
As time giggles in its flight,
For every grain that's spent, you'll see,
Brings forth the joy, pure delight!

Vestiges of the Silent Clock

In quiet corners where whispers laugh,
The silent clock drinks sweet lemonade,
Counting giggles on a staff,
Trading time for charades made.

Silly shadows strut in line,
Ticking on a quiet spree,
In a world where soup is wine,
Time walks backward, fancy-free.

Old gears hum a catchy tune,
Where dances shimmer, twist, and bend,
Each tick is like a fun balloon,
Floating forth with no pretend.

With every pause, the echoes play,
Creating mischief in the air,
So let your heart just laugh away,
As time forgets the weight of care!

Reflections in Starlit Glass

Glimmers of laughter, shadows dance,
Stars giggle softly, in their prance.
Moonbeams tickle, secrets in the night,
Time winks at us, oh what a sight!

Past and present, play tag with glee,
A chandelier of dreams, come see!
Each bubble bursts, with a shimmering yawn,
Tick-tock, tickle, till the break of dawn.

Floating through ages, a carousel spin,
Frogs in tuxedos, let the fun begin!
Jesters of time, in a whimsical race,
Chasing our tails in a giggling chase.

So let us dance under starlit beams,
Sipping on laughter, chasing our dreams.
Reflections shimmer, bright in the glass,
Time takes a bow, and watches us pass.

Chasing Sunset's Embrace

Chasing the giggles, the sun slips low,
Skirts of gold twirling, in twilight's glow.
Clouds wear pajamas, all fluffy and bright,
Dancing with shadows, till they bid goodnight.

Red balloons floating, in the evening air,
Tickling all the stars with a whimsical flair.
The crickets start chirping, a funny old tune,
While shadows play hide and seek with the moon.

Cartwheeling through moments, on a candy cane path,
Spinning in circles, oh what a laugh!
Time's wobbly clock, keeps spinning around,
Where giggles are treasures just waiting to be found.

So let's scurry onward, with joy as our goal,
Chasing the sunset, it tickles our soul.
A canvas of colors, we giggle and grin,
In the embrace of twilight, let the fun begin!

The Portal of Memory

Wandering through laughter, in the hall of the past,
Memories shimmer like bubbles that blast.
Pickles in top hats, join hands with the breeze,
Singing goofy songs, oh what a tease!

Nostalgia floats in on a unicycle ride,
Ducks wearing sandals, take silly strides.
Every snapshot a giggle, a tumble, a flip,
Time's candy-coated moments, a sweet little trip.

Each memory spins, a colorful swirl,
Dancing with squirrels, give it a twirl!
The laughter of years echoes through the hall,
In this portal of fun, come one, come all.

So jump in the frame, let's play and forget,
The weight of the world makes a silly duet.
In this wayward time, we'll savor the jest,
For laughter's the treasure, and joy's the best.

Lanterns in the Mist

Wobbly lanterns shine in the foggy delight,
Marshmallow moonbeams giggle through the night.
Mice in tuxedos, twirling like stars,
Every flicker of light is a promise from Mars.

Time's a cheeky elf, with a skip in his step,
Tossing confetti, no need for prep.
In this misty wonder, fun takes the stage,
As we pirouette forward, turning the page.

Giggling shadows prance on the wall,
With every soft sigh, they rise and they fall.
Echoes of laughter weave tales in the air,
In the swirl of the lanterns, we dance without care.

So let's toast to time, with our drinks full of cheer,
In this scene of delight, we've nothing to fear.
With lanterns and laughter, let's drift and we'll sway,
In the mist of the night, where silliness plays.

Secrets in the Shifting Sands

A crab in a tuxedo, oh so spry,
Dances with a hermit—oh my, oh my!
They spill secrets of the tide,
While seagulls cast their votes, oh what a ride!

Once, a turtle had a wicked plan,
To start a race, oh what a man!
But the finish line got lost in the sea,
And now he's arguing with a bumblebee!

Footprints washed away with a wave's grand call,
What a mess, the beach is a free-for-all!
Yet every grain holds laughter, it seems,
Underneath the sun, they weave silly dreams.

Glimpses Through the Veil of Hours

A clock that ticks in reverse, oh dear,
Makes everyone late—oh what a cheer!
Tea time's a riot, scones start to fly,
As the teapot sings with a jovial sigh.

In the midst of the hourglass, grains tumble down,
While mice don costumes—oh dear, what a frown!
They hold a parade in the empty hall,
With cheese for confetti, oh how they sprawl!

Time slips on banana peels, so absurd,
As whispers turn into giggles unheard.
A calendar flips, pages in a swirl,
Bringing back moments of squirrelly twirls!

Shadows on the Path of Ages

A ghost in a top hat and shoes of red,
Dance through the night, filling hearts with dread.
But who could be scared with such a sight?
He juggles with shadows, full of delight!

The trees gossip loudly, their leaves all a-sway,
While the old oak grumbles, 'Only I can play!'
The branches are tickling, the sun's getting low,
As shadows get silly, putting on a show.

They play hide and seek with the light and the ground,
Creating quite chaos, making their rounds.
With laughter as echoes in the cool evening air,
A comical waltz, oh what a fair!

Time's Unfolding Tapestry

A spider spins threads of moments profound,
Weaving giggles and hiccups all around.
With each little patch, a tale to tell,
Of ketchup that flew and a happy high bell.

Knitting the days with mismatched designs,
Socks on the cat, oh what funny lines!
Each stitch a memory, peek-a-boo plays,
In this fabric of folly, laughter stays.

Time's a jester, with tricks up each sleeve,
Juggling the hours, oh what we believe!
In the grand silly quilt, we find our way,
Smiling at moments that come out to play!

The Keeper of Eternal Secrets

In a dusty room, the keeper sits,
With mismatched socks and numerous wits.
He guards the laughter of ages past,
While sipping tea, oh what a blast!

His hair is wild, like a bird's nest,
Tales of yore, he shares with zest.
A tickle here, a giggle there,
History's secrets transformed to flair.

He whispers jokes from ancient scrolls,
Befuddled looks from curious souls.
Oh, what a sight, the keeper grins,
As laughter echoes, everyone wins!

Through caverns of giggles, he does roam,
His laughter shines, like a dreamy dome.
Eternal secrets, light as a feather,
Unraveling laughter, now and forever.

Portraits in the Gallery of Time

In a hall where portraits giggle loud,
Pouting kings and jesters, quite a crowd.
They wiggle and dance in frames so tight,
Mischief sparkles in the candlelight.

A queen with a cat, both wearing crowns,
Looks like she's plotting to take the towns.
The baker's face, smeared with dough,
Creates a comedic show we all know!

There's a fellow with a nose too large,
Next to a clown who's always in charge.
Their antics echo through the years,
Jokes painted vivid, laughter in tears!

Each brushstroke sways, with humor bright,
In a gallery glowing with pure delight.
Through time they prance, an eternal dance,
Life's funny quirks? It's all just a chance!

Whispers of the Clock

Tick-tock, the clock begins to chuckle,
With every chime, it gives a little shuffle.
It whispers secrets of bygone days,
In a voice that dances in comical ways.

Past moments tickled, they laugh and play,
While the hands spin faster, come what may.
Old lovers giggle, a child with a kite,
All join in the fun, oh what a sight!

The second hand teases the minute's grace,
In the great parade of time's silly face.
A jester's cap on every hour,
Through echoes of time, we share the power.

When midnight strikes, what a ruckus it brings,
With whispers of laughter, the clock surely sings.
Time may be serious, yet it loves to jest,
In its quirky rhythm, we're all truly blessed.

Fragments of Yesterday

Bits of laughter drift like the breeze,
Snowmen in shorts, oh what a tease!
Fragments of yesterday, funny and bright,
Remind us to giggle, even at night.

A runaway balloon, stuck in a tree,
A cat with a hat, as proud as can be.
Old photos smile, with quirky delight,
Reflecting the moments that dance in our sight.

Forgotten lunchboxes, a sandwich from June,
Whispers of snacks lost, we hum a tune.
With memories spinning like tops in the air,
We laugh at the fumbles, the joy we all share.

So here's to the pieces that slip through our grasp,
Each chuckle a treasure, in time we clasp.
Fragments of yesterday shining so clear,
In the gallery of laughter, we hold so dear.

Whispers of the Ancient Door

In a dusty hall, the hinges squeak,
Ghostly jokes from years antique.
Silly secrets spill and sway,
Ancient giggles lead the way.

A clumsy ghost trips on his sheet,
Telling tales, he lands on his feet.
Laughter echoing through the years,
Haunted hiccups turn into cheers.

A grumpy mage forgot his wand,
Baking cookies from a distant pond.
They rise and dance with glee in flight,
Serving snacks to the moon at night.

The door swings wide with a creaky grin,
Letting mischief and fun pour in.
Time can't hold what's meant to play,
In this hallway, it's a holiday.

Echoes from Yesterday's Threshold

A clock that laughs, ticks far too slow,
Counting punchlines, not just the show.
Jokes like daggers, soft and bright,
Pierce the silence, bring delight.

Lambs in socks trip on the floor,
Trying to dance, they knock the door.
With bells that jingle, they twirl around,
Unruly sheep dance to the sound.

A specter's hat flies off in a breeze,
His outdated puns bring you to your knees.
With a wink and a nudge, he tries to rhyme,
The punchline's lost in the sands of time.

Merry shadows that play tag with light,
Wink at the stars, oh what a sight!
Time's a jester, forever in jest,
In this dimension, it's all a fest.

Fragments of Forgotten Yesterdays

In a jar of laughs, memories stew,
Silly pickles in a time-brew.
Each crunch reveals a tale absurd,
Like dancing owls that never heard.

The past swings in, dressed in fun,
A costume party, everyone's a pun.
Time's elastic, like a rubber band,
Stretchy stories that we can't quite stand.

Frogs in top hats, sipping tea,
Discussing when they used to be a bee.
Time keeps changing what we remember,
Lively moments in hot July's ember.

So tip your hat to the wacky past,
With silly hats, we'll have a blast.
Life's just a game that bends and slides,
In these scraps of time, laughter abides.

The Portal of Memory's Gaze

In a gateway made of giggles bright,
Silly shadows dance with delight.
Tickling the dust with each embrace,
In this realm, all wear a grin on their face.

Time-wrinkled socks roam about,
Playing hide and seek without a doubt.
They humor the clocks that tick and tock,
Chasing memories like a playful flock.

Wizards in robes made of candy wrappers,
Casting spells with absurdly loud clappers.
Each chant a jest, a playful tease,
With time-worn laughter carried in the breeze.

With every turn, the door slams shut,
But life spills forth, like a great big glut.
In the playful echoes, we learn to roam,
Finding fun in the realms we call home.

The Colors of Time's Fabric

In a closet full of years, bright hues,
Dancing socks and mismatched shoes.
Lime green laughs at solemn gray,
While polka dots decide to play.

Tattered jeans that once were cool,
Now hide secrets in a pool.
Time's thread unravels, weaves a joke,
A slip of yarn, and then we poke.

The rainbow swirls in cosmic glee,
With every blink, a memory.
Yesterday's giggles ride the breeze,
Faded shirts whisper tales with ease.

Stitched in laughter, patched with love,
Time's quilt fits snug, yet fits like gloves.
Hats from ages past parade,
In this fabric, worries fade.

Countless Echoes

In the hall of forgotten pranks,
Echoes giggle in silly ranks.
Yesterday's voices, all a-squeak,
Crack up the walls, no need to peek.

I heard my childhood self scream,
"Don't eat the glue!", what a dream!
Whispers of laughter float on air,
Rewind the tape, let down your hair.

Pening little secrets in old drawers,
Funny letters from childhood wars.
Each echo, a note in life's grand song,
Makes you wonder where they belong.

Time's giggles stretch from past to now,
Tickling us like a playful cow.
In each laugh, a buried clue,
Countless echoes, life's funny view.

Journeys Beyond the Present

A bicycle built for yesterdays,
Pedals turning in silly ways.
Off we ride, with hats askew,
Chasing clouds and dreams anew.

On streets paved with ice cream scoops,
Dodging giggles and clumsy loops.
We sail on spoons through cosmic streams,
Sipping sunlight, living dreams.

Time travelers in their pajamas,
Stealing starlight from bright dramas.
With every push, we break the mold,
Making mischief, so bold and old.

Mismatched socks are our GPS,
Guiding us through fun excess.
In this wild ride, let's never pause,
For laughter is the best applause.

The Mirror of Ages

Peering in the glassy frame,
Reflections twist, but all the same.
A wrinkled grin with a wink of glee,
"Time's a trickster, just like me!"

A jester dance from days gone by,
Whispers float like butterfly.
Every wrinkle tells a tale,
In this mirror, we can't fail.

Old socks with holes, a badge of cheer,
Tales of laughter woven here.
Smile and jest with every glance,
Time's a silly, fickle dance.

With a twist and a youthful sigh,
We sprout wings and learn to fly.
In every moment, a laugh inside,
Mirrors reflect where fun resides.

Flickering Candles of Memory

In the attic, old hats lay,
Worn by grandpa in his heyday.
He danced like a chicken, I swear,
With a mustache that flowed like the air.

Old photos stacked all around,
Each one a treasure I found.
Grandma's hairdo, a tower so high,
She claimed it was '80s and not just a lie.

We laugh at the fads that have passed,
Like bell-bottoms and mullets, a blast!
But every fond memory, we'd keep,
In the flickering glow while others would sleep.

So let's toast to the quirks of our kin,
With reminders of laughter, let joy begin!
For life's a circus, quirky and spry,
In this big top of memories, oh me, oh my!

A Glimpse into Forever

Peering into the past, what a sight,
Time-warped cats chasing shadows at night.
They swore they could travel, just ask,
But got stuck in a photo booth, oh what a task!

There's Uncle Joe, in a tutu so bright,
Claiming he's a ballerina with all of his might.
He twirls through the years, quite the show,
With a shuffle and giggle, we just can't say no.

A glimpse into moments, some silly, some grand,
Like Dad's cooking that no one can withstand.
The smoke alarm cheers, what a sound!
As we gather the firefighters around!

Memories loop, like a spinning top,
Forever in laughter, we'll never stop.
With mischief and merriment, life whirls by,
In this timeless circus, oh my, oh my!

The Time Traveler's Memoir

Once a time traveler, told tales with flair,
Of socks with sandals, and big fluffy hair.
He whisked us away to the decade of "cool,"
Where everything funky was all the rage at school.

He zipped back to moments all bright,
Where disco was king, and folks danced all night.
We giggled at records that spun and cracked,
As he pulled out a boom box, laughter unpacked.

With each twist of the dial, we'd peek and pry,
At the wacky fashion that made us all sigh.
"Did you have to wear that?" we'd ask in a jest,
And he'd nod with a grin, "Just doing my best!"

So here's to the traveler, spinning the tale,
Of laughter and memories that never go stale.
In his memoir of moments, we know we'll abide,
In this joyful journey, let laughter be our guide.

Secrets Written in Starlight

In the night sky, secrets bloom,
Like popcorn kernels in a living room.
Whispers of stories flicker and dance,
Wrapped in giggles, they take a chance.

Twinkling stars hold tales so grand,
Of toe-tapping fairies and chats with the sand.
One claimed she could out-fly a kite,
But tangled her wings in a fit of delight.

Comets that dated and broke up with glee,
Star-crossed lovers, oh can't you see?
With beaming smiles and witty retorts,
Their cosmic drama is endless, like sports!

So let's share our secrets beneath this light,
With belly laughs echoing through the night.
In the universe's jest, we find our way,
As giggles explode in a cosmic ballet.

Celtic Knots of Time

In a garden of clocks that tick-tock,
A gnome turned to me, said, "What a shock!"
"My beard's grown so long, it's now a vine,"
"I tripped over history, oh how divine!"

Time's tangled in ribbons, bright and bold,
A cat wearing glasses, left out in the cold.
He read me the futures, but fell asleep,
Left me with secrets, I'm bound to keep.

We danced with the daisies, who laughed at the sun,
Time's a merry prankster, oh what fun!
A dragon snored deeply, tucked in a chair,
Dreaming of battles, he swore were quite rare.

Every tick is a giggle, each tock is a laugh,
The past paints the future, like sketches in half.
I tiptoed through ages, on jellybean feet,
In this carnival world, where nonsense is sweet!

Chronicles of the Forgotten

Ah, the tales lost and found, like socks in a dryer,
What happened to history? I might be a liar!
The cavemen were artists, with rocks and with flair,
But their best work restarts from a donut-shaped chair!

Once a knight named Tim rode a llama so fine,
Claimed it was noble, and all were divine.
He jousted with frogs while wearing a crown,
A splash in the moat made him slip and fall down.

Pirates with peg legs played hopscotch at sea,
Exchanging their treasure for cups of hot tea.
Their maps were just doodles, drawn with colored pens,
A quest for the scones with their pixelated friends!

The future looks bright if we keep it absurd,
With punny reflections, life won't be deterred.
Each laugh is a chapter, each smile is a feat,
In this wacky old world, where time has a seat!

A Window to Ages Past

Peering through laughter, I spotted a bear,
Tapping on history, without a care.
His hat was a sundae, his shoes made of pie,
He giggled so loudly, I nearly did cry!

The Romans played chess with a cow as a queen,
In togas of bubble wrap, it was quite the scene.
Julius tripped over, he couldn't quite win,
His toga got tangled—oh, where to begin!

Alec the Inventor built robots to sing,
But only on Mondays, it became quite the thing.
They danced a fine jig, then decided to nap,
A snooze-launch explosion, thumping the map!

Oh, glimpses of madness in all that we see,
Time's just a circus, come join the spree!
With a bounce and a skip, let the echoes arise,
For fun is eternal, beneath open skies!

Starlit Portals

What if the heavens held doors made of cheese?
I'd pop open a window and travel with ease.
With stars for my sidekicks, and comets for flair,
We'd race through the cosmos, with giggles to share!

An alien chef took me out to a feast,
With noodles of stardust, it was quite the beast.
He juggled five planets while frying a sun,
With each bite I took, I knew it was fun!

Through a wormhole, quite wobbly, I took a quick ride,
To meet all the stars who'd previously died.
They showed me their tricks, balloon animals too,
Every shadow a punchline, who knew they could woo?

So let's wrap up our travels with laughter and cheer,
Time's simply a jester, come dance without fear.
In starlit chambers, let our joy be the guide,
For every misadventure should never be denied!

Threads of Ancient Whispers

In a tower of jumbles, old socks and a shoe,
An echo of laughter rings out from the blue.
The roaches play poker, the mice sing a tune,
While time's ever flipping old pages by noon.

A wizard in slippers brews coffee with glee,
Clamoring potions, just what could they be?
The cat keeps a ledger, all secrets she knows,
As the noodles dance 'round in their fanciful throes.

The mirrors reflect the best jokes of the past,
With each ghostly giggle, never meant to last.
Tickle the ivories, a piano that squeaks,
Making music of mischief with calico freaks.

As shadows weave tales that tumble and trip,
The fabric of time's just a jester's skipped quip.
So let's toast our socks, in this Vortex sublime,
To the threads of the whispers, and the jest of old time.

Footprints on Yesterday's Shore

Sandy impressions of clumsy small feet,
Dancing on waves with a rhythm so sweet.
The tides giggle loudly as they roll in and out,
Whispering secrets that bubbles about.

A crab dons a top hat, a sight so absurd,
Waltzing with seagulls, the silliest bird.
They chat about treasure, but it's just a dime,
Minted long ago, but it's still worth the rhyme.

Buried beneath seaweed, a treasure map sketched,
Leads to a sandbox where fortunes are fetched.
But all we discover are toys from the past,
Old flip-flops and snorkels, not meant to last.

So giggle and gather these remnants of play,
The footprints remind us of bright sunny days.
In the playground of ages, let laughter ensure,
Each moment we frolic, the heart's we endure.

The Scribe of the Cosmic Clock

A quill made of stardust, on parchment of space,
Jots down the antics of time's giddy chase.
With fingers so nimble, it spins and it twirls,
While wobbly planets just giggle and swirl.

The hourglass tumbles with grains that can sing,
A chorus of seconds that dance on a string.
The scribe with a wink gives a nod and a laugh,
As tomorrow spills over from yesterday's half.

Backwards they travel, in loops of delight,
Chasing their tales in a roundabout flight.
A bowtie of minutes does a jig with a stare,
As seconds parade in a waltz with flair.

So join in the revel, with candy of light,
As the scribe scrawls the stories that tickle with fright.
In a whirl of giggles, the cosmos takes part,
In the dance of existence, the jester's sweet art.

The Breath of Forgotten Ages

In the attic resides a very odd breeze,
Carrying tales of old quirks and old keys.
The dust starts to hum a whimsical tune,
While moths in top hats dance 'round a balloon.

A ship made of paper sails under the bed,
With pirates of pillows, all full of dread.
They argue and bicker for treasures of fluff,
But what can they find? Just some old, wrinkled stuff.

With gales of laughter, the centuries shout,
While teacups and saucers are spinning about.
In the corners, they giggle, lost snippets of lore,
As the breath of old ages plays peek-a-boo more.

So let's raise our voices to whispers of jest,
For time has a way of spreading its best.
With each crooked giggle from long years ago,
In the dance of the ages, together we flow.

Echoes Beyond the Door

In a world where clocks can giggle,
I found a door that starts to wiggle.
It creaked and laughed, a funny sound,
As past and future spun around.

A pirate danced with a feathered hat,
While dinosaurs swapped jokes with a cat.
I blinked twice, my coffee spilled,
Time's sense of humor, perfectly skilled.

With each tick-tock, a pun was born,
Like lettuce used for a sailor's adorn.
A wizard sneezed, and oh what fun!
The universe cracked up; it's never done.

So when the clock strikes an hour too late,
Join the giggles of time, don't wait.
For every moment that we seize,
Is painted with laughter—oh, what a tease!

The Chrono-Crystal

I found a gem, all shiny and bright,
It whispered jokes in the middle of night.
With every tick of its magical beat,
It juggled moments, a curious feat.

A pterodactyl wore colorful socks,
While Newton balanced cheese on the clocks.
Einstein spilled jam on relativity,
As giggles burst forth with agility.

Time traveled fast on a unicycle,
With a clown juggling marbles in style.
The rules of age bent and flipped,
In this world where laughter has tripped.

So if you seek tales from long ago,
Grab the crystal and dance with the flow.
For in this madness where fun reigns high,
History laughs, oh my, oh my!

Secrets of the Hourglass

In an hourglass filled with grains of cheer,
The whispers of time tickled my ear.
Sandmen giggled with grains of humor,
While moments paraded as silly rumor.

I saw a fish in a bow tie and suit,
Dancing with ants in time's grand pursuit.
Each hour that passed, a joke was spun,
From what once was lost to what's yet begun.

A walrus rode on a skateboard with flair,
As laughter echoed in the salty air.
With each shake of the hourglass tight,
Silly stories took to flight.

So if you find secrets trapped in glass,
Know laughter is the best that will pass.
For in the sands of time, oh so fine,
You'll find chuckles hidden—yours and mine!

Shadows of the Past

In shadows where time likes to sneak,
I met a ghost who couldn't speak.
But with a wink, and a cheeky pout,
He cracked a joke and spun about.

Flappers danced with a clatter of shoes,
While cavemen tried to sing the blues.
Hilarity spilled from every nook,
As time's old laughter played the book.

Napoleon tripped over his own hat,
While Cleopatra giggled at that.
History bent, twisted with glee,
In a time where laughter is the key!

So if you wander through the past's embrace,
Join in the fun, keep up the pace.
For every shadow hides a quip,
In the dance of time's hilarious trip!

The Box of Yesterdays

In a box of past delight,
Old socks dance in moonlight.
They giggle with every sway,
In a silly, faded play.

Forgotten jokes take a stand,
With invisible slapstick brand.
They tumble out with a cheer,
As my pet goldfish rolls a tear.

The snacks are stale but taste so grand,
Like time's own weird and wacky band.
Old toys laugh and plot a heist,
Stealing memories, oh how nice!

So here we sit, in laughter's throng,
With yesterdays that feel so wrong.
Yet every moment, light and bright,
Reminds us that it's all alright!

Fragments of a Forgotten Symphony

Notes of laughter fill the air,
As socks perform a silly flair.
Each squeak a tune, a silly rhyme,
Creating chaos out of time.

The cat conducts with fervent meows,
While the dog plays drums with clumsy paws.
The chairs all join with clinks and clatters,
As time forgets what truly matters.

A trumpet made from grandma's pie,
Blows out tunes that dance and fly.
While jellies jam against the wall,
In a concert that makes no sense at all.

So let's embrace this quirky sound,
In this symphony profound.
With laughter loud and joy unbound,
In fragments lost, true gold is found!

The Path of Shimmering Stars

On a path paved with silly dreams,
Stars slip and slide, or so it seems.
They twinkle with a winking eye,
Inviting us to laugh and cry.

A comet trips and does a spin,
While planets giggle, sensing win.
They race through night with grace so fine,
Leaving trails of glittery wine.

Aliens wave from wobbly ships,
Offering snacks of odd-shaped chips.
A moonbeam slips, so let's all cheer,
For cosmic jokes brought ever near!

So let us dance among the gleams,
Where laughter sprinkles on our dreams.
For every star that tumbles down,
Brings humor to this merry town!

Timeless Wishes

Wishes wrapped in bubble gum,
Float along, a wacky hum.
They bounce around with silly pouts,
Turning frowns to cheerful shouts.

Each wish a trickster in disguise,
Socks that tickle and surprise.
A lifetime packed in a rubber band,
That stretches wide like time was planned.

Old dreams in flip-flops stroll with zest,
Seeking mischief, never rest.
In this timeless, playful spree,
The present laughs at history!

So toss a wish, let laughter flow,
In moments lost, let antics grow.
For life's a joke that's never lame,
In timeless fun, we stake our claim!

Reveries of a Timeless Dream

A wizard sneezed, the clock it froze,
Time stood still, as laughter rose.
Cats in hats danced all around,
While echoes of secrets giggled loud.

A chicken crossed the cosmic street,
To find a worm with four left feet.
Tick-tock said the silly bird,
But no one really heard a word.

In slippers soft, the shadows prance,
In a waltz with dreams, a merry dance.
Socks mismatched, they twirl and spin,
While clocks just grin at all the din.

With candy clouds and rivers bright,
We chase our echoes through the night.
Time's a jester, playful and spry,
Winking gently as the hours fly.

Lanterns of Lost Light

A lantern's glow, a giggle bright,
Chased shadow beasts that took to flight.
The moon got lost, a hapless spark,
In a game of tag, they roamed the dark.

Old shoes creaked with tales to tell,
Of rubber ducks that splashed so well.
A glowing fish wore fancy hats,
And laughed at dogs with tiny bats.

Through skies of pink and polka dots,
We swirl with glee, oh, what a plot!
A picnic basket filled with cheese,
Sat on a cloud, swaying in the breeze.

A tumbleweed wore spectacles,
While chortles echoed, oh, so flexible.
Each moment winked, a riddle spun,
In lantern light, we chase the fun.

The Echo Chamber of Yore

In an echo chamber, voices play,
They dance and tickle in a silly way.
A talking spoon debated with a fork,
While shadows plotted a game of cork.

Jellybeans bounced in old old chairs,
Whispering secrets of forgotten flares.
The walls dripped stories, oh so neat,
Of dancing mice with tap-shoe feet.

A time machine made of crayons bright,
Took us across the ticklish night.
Where jellyfish wore polka-dots,
And all the fish exchanged their thoughts.

In giggling echoes, the past appeared,
Mistaking time for what's revered.
A funfair riddle wrapped in rhyme,
In chambers vast, we roast the time.

Threads of Light and Shadow

In the web of night, shadows tease,
While light threads dance with graceful ease.
A little ghost wears sparkly shoes,
Poking fun as it strolls the views.

Lollipop trees sprout candy spritz,
While giggling squirrels do silly flips.
A time traveler forgot the way,
Got stuck in a loop of yesterday.

Butterflies burst from brilliant blooms,
Whispering laughter in playful rooms.
Each creature hops on time's wobbly ride,
In circles and spirals, we all take pride.

With laughter stitched in every seam,
We craft a patchwork of joy supreme.
In the threads of light and shadow's chase,
The world spins round, a funny place.

The Dance of Hours

Tick-tock with a silly grin,
Time steps out, wears a spin.
Two left feet, can't hold a beat.
Chasing minutes on trampoline feet.

A waltz where seconds trip and fall,
Hours giggling, having a ball.
Laughter echoes in the clock's face,
Every tick a moments' race.

Unruly hands start a parade,
Fleeting moments' masquerade.
Round and round, what a sight,
Now the minutes are in flight!

But worry not, they'll return fast,
Dancing tales of a ludicrous past.
So grab a partner for this ride,
In the dance where time does slide!

Dreams Entwined in Time

In a dream, I lost my shoe,
Time stumbles by, oh, what a view!
A cat in a hat, a dog on skates,
Chasing stars through time's funny gates.

Tea with a rabbit, clocks made of cheese,
Time says, "Come, if you please!"
A herd of sheep, counting them high,
While the hours wink, oh my, oh my!

A watch that squeaks, with legs that dance,
Tickling moments, take a chance!
Dreams twirl round, never leave,
In this time where we believe.

So skip through the dreams, don't be shy,
Time's the friend who won't say goodbye.
Join the giggles, laughter's chime,
Let's just waltz into the rhyme!

The Memento of Yesterday

Yesterday wore a silly hat,
Sipping tea with a dancing cat.
Memories twirling in the breeze,
Ticklish moments under the trees.

A snapshot where giggles collide,
Time's on a rollercoaster ride.
With polka dots and stripes so bold,
Yesterday's stories never grow old.

Jumping jacks at the break of dawn,
Wearing mischief like a fawn.
A photo booth with an ominous grin,
Chasing the past where laughs begin.

So treasure this quirky mess,
In the memento of happy excess.
For time's a trickster, bright and gay,
Slide into memories, come what may!

The Canvas of Eternity

Painting time with a floppy brush,
Colors mingle in a silly rush.
A canvas bright, faces all goofy,
Creating moments, oh so moody!

Picture frames sing with laughter's glow,
Chasing rainbows only time can show.
Each stroke creates a whimsical tale,
In this world where tick-tocks sail.

A canvas splashed with cotton candy,
Time's giggles are sweet and dandy.
Sprinkles of joy, dotting the scene,
Brushy rain clouds, paint my dream!

So dance with whimsy, don't ever cease,
In the vibrant canvas, find your peace.
For every smile is a stroke divine,
A masterpiece that sparkles with time!

Windows to Forgotten Dreams

In the attic, dust takes flight,
Old toys chuckle, what a sight!
A rubber duck and teddy bear,
Wonder where's their time to share?

A clock once ticked in vibrant glee,
Wound too tight, now it won't agree.
It tells the time, or so it claims,
But really, it's just playing games.

Postcards from the past come by,
Funny hats and big blue sky.
The dreams we had, they tease and jibe,
Were we ever really that tribe?

So peek inside that box of cheer,
Invite the past to hang out here.
With laughter loud and stories grand,
Let's dance like we did back then, hand in hand!

The Tapestry of Moments

A quilt of laughs, stitched with care,
Each patch a tale, a little rare.
Coffee spills and ice cream drips,
Weaving dreams with silly quips.

A moment here—a sneeze, a cheer,
Frogs in top hats, the news we hear.
No need for grandeur, just some fun,
As jokes and jests get swiftly spun.

Time's little jester rolls the dice,
Dancing socks, how very nice!
Elder winks, a kid's wild grin,
Who knew that chaos held the win?

Pluck a thread, let laughter rise,
And find the giggles in surprise.
So weave it all, both old and new,
This tapestry is stitched with you!

Glimpses of Lost Tomorrows

In the garden, weeds wear crowns,
Dandelions in silly gowns.
Tomorrow's plans have gone to play,
Perhaps they'll join us some sweet day.

Frogs wearing glasses croak their news,
With every hop, they spill their views.
Jellybeans and gummy bears,
Lost tomorrows hide in pairs.

A pot of gold? Just chocolate bars,
Tomorrow's dreams tucked in jars.
Poking fun, the clock just grins,
While inside it, laughter spins.

So grab a spoon and join the feast,
For lost tomorrows aren't deceased.
They dance in shadows, laugh and tease,
Let whimsy float upon the breeze!

The Timekeeper's Tale

A fussy clock in top hat waits,
With punny puns and twisted fates.
"Don't rush me!" it insists with glee,
"I'm far too busy sipping tea!"

A calendar, all wrinkled and wise,
Winks, as if it spins bright lies.
Sundays are napping, Fridays rave,
Time is just a silly wave.

An hourglass ticks its sandy snore,
"Faster, faster!" we implore.
While squirrels debate the daily grind,
Timekeeper giggles; isn't it blind?

The tale unfolds with laughter spry,
Tick-tock, tick-tock, oh my, oh my!
Chronicles of jest, a joyous feast,
In every moment, we are released!

Timelines Untangled

In a clock that clicks in reverse,
I danced with dinosaurs - oh, what a curse!
They thought I was a tasty treat,
But I just wanted to tap my feet.

With cavemen drawing on walls so wide,
I asked them to join my crazy ride.
They threw me a bone but I lost my shoes,
We ended up in the news - can you guess the views?

I zipped to the '80s, all neon and hair,
People with shoulder pads filled the air.
They thought I was retro, a blast from the past,
But my time machine runs out of gas fast!

Now I sit in a loop, watching time unwind,
Trading my stories with folks undefined.
From giggling cavemen to disco ball dreams,
This winding path is not what it seems!

The Lost Pages of Eternity

In a book that flips through ages so grand,
I stumbled on recipes from a distant land.
One called for moonbeams, another for stars,
I could've fed all my friends on Mars!

The pages flipped fast, like fish out of water,
Eating history like it's a banquet platter.
A sip from a potion, I started to float,
Toasting with Einstein in a cosmic boat!

I met Shakespeare, he whispered a line,
"Are we all just characters trying to shine?"
I quipped back, "Good sir, let us be bold,
What's better than stories that never grow old?"

In this library where giggles abound,
Lost pages of laughter are all that I've found.
I'll never return, I'll live in this rhyme,
Eating history's antics, one page at a time!

A Journey Through the Ages

I hopped on a chariot, full speed ahead,
Chasing a chicken that dreams up some bread.
Flipping through time like a pancake chef,
Landing in Rome, I yelled, "Save me a Jeff!"

In medieval times, knights wore such flair,
But they couldn't dance - oh, what a scare!
With my funky moves and a disco ball,
I turned jousting knights into a dance-off brawl!

The Renaissance fair had me feeling quite chic,
Doodling in paint while the artists peek.
But a rogue time traveler stole my last snack,
Now I'm chasing history - I want my treat back!

So I march through the ages, with laughter and glee,
Making friends with jesters, that's the key!
Each step may be silly, but I'm having a blast,
In this wacky adventure, I'm never quite last!

The Realm of Echoing Footsteps

In a hallway where echoes play hide and seek,
I stumbled on secrets that wanted to speak.
With a giggle and jump, I danced down the hall,
Where footprints of laughter began their enthrall.

I dodged past the pharaohs with wigs like a sun,
Their fashion advice? Just have some fun!
I twirled past the Romans, in sandals and sails,
Who tried to out-chuckle my favorite tales.

In shadows of history, I stumbled upon,
A castle where jokes were feared to be gone.
I yelled, "Let's laugh, let's tickle the past!"
And soon echoes of giggles erupted so fast!

Now I prance through this realm with a jester's delight,
Time tickling laughter, oh, what a sight!
Every footstep I take sends ripples of cheer,
In this funny parade, everyone's welcome here!

Beyond the Threshold of Eternity

I found a door, all shiny and bright,
Thought I might peek, what a silly delight.
Saw a dodo bird, wearing a hat,
It winked and said, "What do you think of that?"

A turtle raced, just for show,
Said, "I'm late for a date, don't you know?"
I laughed so hard, I nearly fell,
Into a time where laughter could swell.

A clock with legs danced by my side,
Singing a tune, with great pride.
It said, "Time flies, but I take it slow,"
"Care for a ride, you'll never outgrow?"

With every tick, a new scene appears,
Frogs in tuxedos, sipping cold beers.
I waved goodbye, hopping away,
Time's funny tricks made my day!

The Scrolls of Chronos' Gift

At the library of ages, I took a peek,
Found scrolls that whispered, oh so unique.
One said, "Repeat, you'll forget the line,"
The other chuckled, "Cinnamon's divine!"

I read of knights who tripped on their swords,
And wizards who conjured hilarious hoards.
"Why'd the chicken cross?" the scrolls all asked,
"To get to the other side!" was the task.

A squirrel in armor juggled some acorns,
Said, "Royal rodents must wear old adorns!"
These scrolls of wonders, a real laugh fest,
Bet you a dime they're better than jest.

As I left the tales of past and gone,
I felt the giggles, like a magic wand.
Who knew history had such flair?
I'll read again, without a care!

When Seconds Speak in Silence

I sat alone, with seconds to share,
They whispered jokes, without a care.
"Did you hear the one about the clock?"
"It couldn't stop ticking, loud as a rock!"

A minute came by, wore a silly grin,
Said, "Time flies when you're watching the spin."
"Why so serious?" asked the hourglass,
"Just holding on, let it all pass!"

I joined the party, with seconds and more,
They danced to rhythms, I couldn't ignore.
Tick-tock, they laughed, in a soft ballet,
Turning the silence into a play.

As shadows stretched, the hours grew bright,
I learned to laugh at the silliest sight.
In the rhythm of time, I found my cheer,
When seconds speak, laughter draws near!

Time's Veiled Narrative

In a land where minutes wore capes of flair,
Stories unfolded, oh dear, what a pair!
A jester once juggled both day and night,
Said, "Comedic relief makes time feel just right!"

The sun and the moon swapped tales by the sea,
Of silly antics and lost memory.
"I spun the stars," said the sun with a grin,
"And I tickled the dusk as it traveled within!"

A time-traveling cat played a guitar,
Sang about travelers lost by a bar.
"Why fret over time?" asked the clever beast,
"Let laughter be the very first feast!"

As shadows danced with giggles so true,
Chronicles of joy, coming to you.
In this mystical dance, I found my rhyme,
Laughter shall echo beyond every chime!

The Timekeeper's Secrets

In a room with dozens of clocks,
I found an old cat wearing socks.
He winked at me, said, "Time's a joke!"
I laughed so hard, I nearly choked!

The seconds tiptoed, all in a rush,
While minutes giggled, causing a hush.
With each tick-tock, I danced with glee,
As time played tricks, just like a spree!

Lurking behind a dusty old shelf,
Was a calendar, acting like an elf.
It flipped its pages with giddy flair,
Whispering secrets like a mischievous heir.

In this madcap world, I felt so bright,
As clocks cracked jokes that tickled my sight.
With each riddle, the hours flew by,
Leaving me grinning, oh me, oh my!

A Passageway of Faded Dreams

In a hallway of dreams where shadows play,
I stumbled on socks that led me astray.
They whispered of journeys to lands of cheese,
Where time is fleeting and laughter's a breeze.

One door was painted bright yellow,
A sign read, "Enter, you silly fellow!"
Inside were fairies on roller skates,
Who giggled and danced and opened the gates.

I found a chair that giggled with glee,
It told me tales of a crab on a spree.
With every whisper from walls stained with time,
I couldn't help chuckling, feeling sublime!

Faded dreams tickled my wandering mind,
Each moment a treasure, a surprise to find.
With a wink and a laugh, I stepped right through,
To chase after memories, both old and new!

Unlocking the Echoes of Existence

In a cavern where echoes tickled the air,
I found a door with a mischievous glare.
It creaked open wide with a silly sound,
And time tripped over, tumbling down.

Old boots were chatting about last night's dance,
They laughed at their laces, what a romanced chance!
Each echo a giggle, a laugh from the past,
Wishing for moments that just wouldn't last.

I spotted a clock that rolled on the floor,
It looked at me, then it begged for more.
"Can you hold my hand?" it chimed with delight,
So we hopped through the echoes, oh what a sight!

And with each jump, we howled and we spun,
As time whispered softly, "Aren't we just fun?"
With echoes of laughter, we danced and we played,
In this silly realm where no one dismayed!

The Dance of Eternity Unraveled

In a ball of confetti, I spotted a clock,
Dressed as a dancer with shoes made of rock.
It twirled and it spun, like a whirlwind of glee,
While time wobbled, asking, "Won't you dance with me?"

The whole room was jiving, every second aflame,
A mosh pit of laughter, no one felt shame.
With tick-tocks that foxtrotted through space,
I lost track of minutes in this wild place!

The moon moonwalked, and the sun took a bow,
While hours slapped five—what a sight to endow!
With each silly step, time tickled my toes,
And I giggled so hard, I almost fell, who knows?

As the dance came to close, the laughter rang clear,
In a universe spun from delight and cheer.
With time as my partner, I twirled to my fate,
In this whimsical waltz, where no one was late!

Mesmerizing Moments

In a realm where giggles gleam,
Time skips like a playful dream.
Watches tick in silly rhymes,
Chasing shadows, making crimes.

Mice wear hats, they toast with cheese,
Dancing at their own unease.
Cookies vanish, crumbs collide,
In this world, we laugh and hide.

Grandmas race on roller skates,
Sharing tales of ancient fates.
Time hops like a joyful bunny,
Making memories, oh so funny!

So let us twirl in moments blithe,
When giggles rule and worries writhe.
In this bright, whimsical show,
We find the joy in each tableau.

The Garden of Ancients

In a garden where past blooms sprout,
Elders gossip, there's never a doubt.
Snakes play cards with wise old trees,
While daisies chuckle in the breeze.

Gnomes argue over a missing sock,
While trolls tickle clocks 'til they're in shock.
Bees wear glasses, acting so grand,
Buzzing tales of a magical land.

Old roots share stories, oh what a treat,
Of dances danced on giant beet.
Laughter echoes like summer rain,
In this garden, go insane!

So come and wander this silly space,
Where every petal holds a playful face.
Time flows backward, isn't it neat?
Where ancient mischiefs can't be beat!

Reflected Faces in Silver

In mirrors where giggles reflect,
Silly faces, what to expect?
Wink at the past, it winks right back,
With hairdos made from a snack!

Frogs wear crowns, and cats wear shoes,
In a dance-off, they cannot lose.
Time's a jester with tricks up its sleeve,
Making all the wise ones believe.

Laughter bounces off polished glass,
As shadows giggle; they're having class.
Watch out for ducks that quack in tune,
Synchronized with the man on the moon!

So peek inside, what do you see?
A world that hums with glee and spree.
In reflected faces, find the cheer,
For every tick, it's time we steer!

Messages from the Old Clock

Tick-tock says the old wall clock,
Spinning tales of a twisted sock.
At midnight, it does a little jig,
And hums along with a dancing pig.

Hands go backward, in need of a snack,
As squirrels plan a raccoon attack.
Time's a prankster in a tall hat,
Whispering secrets of a sunny cat.

Every chime brings bursts of laughter,
Making mischief a delightful blaster.
Pigeons wear suits, looking so sly,
As time flutters past with a winked eye.

Oh, listen close to the clock's riddle,
When seconds dance, and giggles whittle.
So find your joy, don't let it flee,
In the funny tick-tock jubilee!

Keys to Yesterday's Heart

In a pocket, I found a door,
With rusty hinges, it made me snore.
I peeked inside, what did I find?
A dance-off with my old behind!

The socks wore stripes, I couldn't believe,
I laughed so hard, I might just pee.
A party where no one ever aged,
We all just sang, forever engaged!

My grandma was breakdancing, quite a sight,
While my dad attempted to take flight.
Oh, the memories, funny and sweet,
With jelly beans stuck to our feet!

So here I go, back to the present,
With giggles and glee, my heart is crescent.
Those keys to yesterday's silly art,
Unlocking joy in every heart!

Lost in the Clockwork

A tick-tock here, a tick-tock there,
I tripped on gears and fell with flair.
The clock hands danced, oh what a show,
They tickled my nose, made me go 'whoa!'

I met a rabbit with time to spare,
He wore a top hat and a wild stare.
We raced through moments, but who was fast?
We ended up tripping on a memory blast!

Grandfather clocks were having tea,
Discussing life, just you and me.
With scones and jam, oh what a feat,
I wonder if time's gluten-free treat!

So here I am, with sand in my shoe,
Lost in a world that feels so new.
With laughter echoing in every tick,
I turn my daydream into a trick!

Corridors of Enchanted Time

In corridors where shadows play,
I wandered through the fray of fray.
Each door I opened brought a laugh,
Like finding jokes in the aftermath!

A dinosaur taught me how to slide,
While robots hosted a dance-off wide.
I spun with fairies, oh what fun!
Dressed up as a pizza, I was the one!

Past lives in silly costumes swirled,
In this odd place my heart unfurled.
With each funny tale, we all did cheer,
Time stood still, a laugh-filled sphere!

So when you walk those halls of bliss,
Don't worry, I promise you won't miss.
With giggles echoing through every chime,
It's just the magic of enchanted time!

The Dance of Celestial Patterns

Stars lined up for a quirky dance,
With meteors giving them a chance.
I joined a waltz with the moonlit glow,
Tripped on my feet, oh what a show!

Galaxies swirling in sequins bright,
Made my head spin, what a delightful sight.
Comets flew by with a flash and a wink,
Dancing on air, made my heart sink!

Planets were laughing, spinning in place,
While I twirled out, lost in the space.
However, I stumbled through the Milky Way,
Falling headfirst into a cosmic spray!

So if you ever catch a glimpse so rare,
Of celestial beings without a care,
Join the dance and feel the rhyme,
In the spectacle of silly time!

www.ingramcontent.com/pod-product-compliance
Lightning Source LLC
Chambersburg PA
CBHW062109280426
43661CB00086B/376